RIDDLES OF RULE: A COLLECTION OF ESSAYS ON POWER, POLICY & POLITICAL THEORY

HASAN RAZI KAZMI

With special thanks to my family

who pressed me to write this book,

and helped me every step of the way

By the Same Author

AZAD: A Journey Towards Independence.

IN THE LOVING MEMORY
OF

SAYED MOHAMMAD RAZI KAZMI

SAYED RAZI HASAN KAZMI

SAYED SAFDAR ABBAS KAZMI

CONTENT

<u>Preface</u>

This is my first attempt at writing a textbook on Political Science, introducing the disciplines of Political Theory, International Relations, and Governance and Policy Making. In writing this book, my aim is to present my personal views on a range of topics in a concise form. My book can serve as a textbook for introducing these topics and aims to make Political Science interesting for people from all backgrounds. I have always feared that people prefer to get information on crucial topics from unreliable social media sources rather than reading and analysing theory, which I believe is extremely dangerous and should be avoided.

The following chapters are divided into three sections: Political Theory, Global Politics and International Relations, and Governance and Policy Making. I have tried to present complex issues in a newer and simpler form, offering a progression of ideas without implying that my views are better simply because they are newer. While I have views on most subjects covered in this book, I assume the role of a writer is not to primarily praise or condemn but to present arguments fairly.

Chapter 1 (Political Philosophy) discusses John Stuart Mill, Socialism, and Nehru's Secularism in detail. Chapter 2 (Global Politics and International Relations) examines characteristic topics such as

Feminist Perspective on IR, Decolonization in South East Asia, China's Rise, World-Systems Theory, the Treaty of Westphalia, and the End of the Cold War. Chapter 3 (Governance and Policy Making) covers India-centric topics like Land Reforms and the Green Revolution, the Changing Nature of the Indian Party System, Powers and Functions of MPs, and the Right to Information Act.

All books are, in one way or another, multi-authored. Having studied Political Science for six years, I have exchanged ideas with many teachers and friends, making it difficult to discern where my thinking begins and theirs ends. Listing all those who have influenced my views over the years would be impossible. I would like to thank teachers like Dr. Z. Siddiqui and Mrs. R. Sharma, who have greatly helped me by explaining basic concepts and preventing silly mistakes. Long and tiring arguments with friends like Sami Ahmed and Yasir Saeed Alvi have also shaped many of my views over the years.

HASAN RAZI KAZMI

Tehsil Fatehpur, Barabanki, 2024

ACKNOWLEDGEMENTS

As I pen these words of gratitude, my heart swells with love, respect, and appreciation for those who have illuminated my journey. First and foremost, I am forever indebted to my guiding light, my elder brother, Bhaiyya – a beacon of wisdom, integrity, and compassion. Your unwavering support and sage counsel have been the North Star that has navigated me through life's triumphs and tribulations. You embody excellence, and I strive to emulate your remarkable example. To my beloved sister, Bitiya, I offer my deepest thanks. Your selfless dedication, unwavering encouragement, and generous spirit have been a constant source of strength, empowering me to pursue my dreams with confidence and determination.

To my loved ones, friends, and all those who have touched my life in meaningful ways, I offer my heartfelt thanks. Your presence and support have made a profound impact on my life and work. Your love, laughter, and tears have inspired me, motivated me, and pushed me to reach for the stars. I am grateful for the late-night conversations, the early morning coffee breaks, and the countless moments in between, where we shared our hopes, fears, and dreams.

I am also grateful for the lessons learned, the challenges overcome, and the growth experienced throughout this journey. I have discovered the power of perseverance, the beauty of vulnerability, and the strength of community. I have learned to embrace my flaws, celebrate my successes, and find joy in the journey.

In conclusion, I want to express my deepest gratitude to everyone who has believed in me and in the transformative magic of stories. Your support, encouragement, and love have made this book possible, and I am forever grateful. Thank you for being part of my journey, for walking alongside me, and for sharing in my joy. I hope this book will touch your heart and inspire your mind.

Thank you all!

<u>List of Abbreviations</u>

- IR - International Relations.

- NGO - Non-Governmental Organisation.

- USD - United States Dollar.

- BRI – Border Road Organisation.

- PLA – People's Liberation Army.

- INSTC – International North-South Transport Corridor.

- QUAD – Quadrilateral Alliance.

- BRICS – Brazil, Russia, India, China, South Africa.

- USSR – Union of Soviet Socialist Republics.

- APEC – Asia-Pacific Economic Cooperation.

- ASEAN – Association of South-East Asian Nations.

- AFTA – ASEAN Free Trade Agreement.

- NAFTA – North-American Free Trade Agreement.

- PIF – Public Investment Fund.

- SCO – Shanghai Cooperation Organisation.

- G7 – Group of Seven.

- G20 – Group of Twenty.

- EU – European Union.

- SAARC – South-Asian Association of Regional Cooperation.

- OPEC – Organisation of Petroleum Exporting Countries.

- CHRI – Commonwealth Human Rights Initiatives.

- BSP – Bahujan Samaj Party.

- DMK – Dravida Munnetra Kazhagam.

- INDIA – Indian National Developmental Inclusive Alliance.

- NDA – National Democratic Alliance.

- TDP – Telugu Desam Party.

- JDU – Janata Dal United.

- MP – Members of Parliament.

- MOSPI – Ministry of Statistics and Programme Implementation.

- MPLAD – Member of Parliament Local Are Development.

- CAG – Comptroller and Auditor General.

- RTI – Right to Information Act.

- CIC – Central Information Commission.

- SCIC – State Chief Information Commissioner.

Political Philosophy: - <u>John Stuart Mill</u>

John Stuart Mill was a renowned English philosopher, economist and politician who made significant contributions to the field of ethics, political philosophy, and social theory. His idea of liberty, particularly his defence of individual freedom, have had a lasting impact on political philosophy.

Mill's philosophy is grounded in the belief that individuals have the right to live their lives as they see fit, free from extreme constraints imposed by the society or the state. He was a strong advocate for individual freedom and argued that the only legitimate purpose of the state is to protect the individual, his life a freedom.

J.S. Mill's concept of Liberty: -

Mill's concept of liberty is based on the principle that every individual should be free to as they please, as far as their actions do not harm others. He argued, people should be free to pursue their own goals and desires without any interference and the state should only intervene when necessary to the rights of others.

He strongly believed that individual freedom was essential for creativity, human development, and flourishing. According to him, societies that stifled individual freedom were doomed to stagnation and decline.

Mill argued that a society which values individual freedom would be more innovative, expressive, and dynamic than the one which restricted individual freedom. His ideas and thoughts are rooted in his belief that individuals have an inherent right to live their lives as they see fit.

Mill's ideas on Minority Rights: -

J.S. Mill was a strong and staunch supporter of minorities rights and argued that minority groups should be protected from the tyranny of the majority. Mill believed that the majority could use its power to oppress majority could use its power to oppress minority groups and the state had a duty to protect the rights of minorities. He believed the state should intervene, even if it meant overriding the wishes of the majority.

Critique of Mill's ideas of Liberty: -

While Mill's ideas have been very influential, they have been subject to criticisms. One critique of Mill's 'harm principle' is that, its too vague and difficult to apply in practice. He argued that individuals should be free to do as they please, as far as their actions do not harm others. It can be difficult to determine when an individual's actions harm others and when they do not, leading to uncertainty about when the state should intervene to protect the rights of others.

Mill's understanding of liberty is too individualistic and does not adequately consider the collective interests of society. Critics argue that Mill's emphasis on the individual may lead to a conflict with wider society and state has the responsibility of promoting the common good. His ideas of liberty are rooted in a western liberal tradition and do not adequately address the concerns of non-western countries.

Despite these criticism Mill's ideas of freedom, individualism remain influential, particularly his advocacy of minority rights and his belief in individual freedom. His advocacy of minority rights, and his concept of liberty have had a lasting impact on the tradition pf Political Philosophy.

John Stuart Mill

Political Philosophy: -
<u>Socialism in Depth</u>

The word 'socialism' is derived from a Latin word *'sociare,'* meaning to combine or share. Its earliest known usage was is 1827 in Britain, in an issue of the co-operative magazine. By early 1830's, the followers of *Robert Owen* (1771-1825) in Britain, and *Saint Simon* (1760-1858) in France had started to refer their beliefs as 'socialism' and by 1840's the term was familiar in a range of industrialised countries, notably France, Belgium, and the German States.

The character of socialism was influenced by harsh and often inhumane conditions in which the working lass lived and worked. The *'Laissez-faire'* (non-interference) policies of the 19th century gave factory owners a free hand in setting wage limits and working conditions. As a result, early socialists often sought a radical, even revolutionary alternative to industrial capitalism. For instance, *Charles Fourier* (1772-1837) and *Robert Owen* in Britain advocated the establishment of utopian communities based upon cooperation, love and empathy rather than competition and greed.

German philosophers, *Karl Marx* (1818-1883) and *Friedrich Engles* (1820-1895), developed a more complex and systematic theory which claimed to uncover the laws History and proclaimed a revolutionary overthrow of capitalism was inevitable.

In late 19th century, the character of socialism was transformed by a gradual improvement of the working-class living conditions and the advancement of political democracy. In the advanced working societies of western Europe, it became increasingly difficult to continue to see the working class as a revolutionary force. By the First World War, the socialist world was clearly divided between those, usually in more backward countries such as Russia, which proclaimed continuing need for the revolution.

The Bolshevik Revolution or October-November Revolution of 1917 entrenched this split, Revolutionary Socialists, following the example of *Lenin* and the *Bolsheviks*, usually adopted the title 'communists', while reform socialists retained the name 'socialists' or social democrats.

Features: -

a) **More emphasis on society than on Individual** – Socialism places more emphasis on the society or collectively than on the individual. It subordinates the individual interest to the higher interests of the society at large.

b) **Abolition of private ownership of means of production and their management for social good** – In his book, *'Introduction to Modern Political Theory,'* Professor *Cyrill Edwin Mitchinson Joad* (1881-1953) says that there are important elements of socialism are common to all socialist schools.
These are: -

1) The private ownership of the means of production to be abolished with this objective, important industries, and services to be brought under public ownership and control.

2) Industry is to be carried on for the purpose of ministering to the needs of the community and not with the aim of making profit for the individuals; the extant and character of production to be determined, therefore not by anticipation of profit but by the consideration of social services, which is at present thwarted by the capitalisation of industry to be

substituted for the incentives of private profit.

c) **Opposition to Capitalism** – Socialism is opposed to capitalism as the later is based on the principle of profit making and not on the increased production for the sake of common good. Capitalism, leads to unequal distribution of wealth among the different classes. It wants production to be carried on in accordance with needs of the society and the distribution to be carried on in accordance with the principle of social justice.

d) **Elimination of Competition** – Socialism stands for the elimination of competition because it leads to a harmful waste, which can be easily avoided socialists one of the opinions that under the capitalist system of production, there is competition for the sake profits alone. There are no monopolies such as cartels, trusts, and corporations which indulge in unhealthy competition.

e) **Abolition of Private Enterprise** – Socialism believes in abolition private enterprises and private property. Socialists aim at transforming private enterprise into public and collective enterprise.

f) **Equality (basis of socialism)** – Socialism stands for equality and aims at establishing greater equality for all. They intend to reduce inequality to such an extent that the divisions and boundaries between the working class and upper class are erased.

g) **Socialist view of the State** – Different socialists believe in the formation of a stateless society. They consider the state to be an instrument of exploitation and compulsion. As such they want to do away with the state. They advocate a withering away of the state. This has been their approach right from the days of Saint Simon.

Criticism: -

a) **Socialism can lead to authoritarianism** – In the first instance it is pointed out by the critics that socialism stands for authoritarianism and bureaucratic control on a wider scale. State's control over the means of wealth production and management will lead to corruption. Socialism expects much from the government or the social organisations which they want to set up.

b) **Impractical** – Socialism can fail in practice as social and economic inequality which are present in each society are so widespread that socialism cannot really remove these. Hence, socialism cannot really remove these.

c) **State cannot effectively administer industries** – It is now a fact that the state may not be able to manage industries as efficiently and effectively as a private enterprise. Most government employees do not take interest in their work.

d) **Private Property is not Evil** – Socialism aims at abolishing private property. Some critics point out that private property is a great incentive. If this incentive is taken away from the people, they will not work whole-heartedly. This was proved to be a fact when Mao allowed some form of private property to the collective farmers as an incentive for working hard.

e) **Socialism negates Liberty** – It limits individual and personal liberty. Socialists make loud claims that their system will bring about real freedom and security to the individual. It will turn workers wage slaves.

f) **Socialism limits progress and development** – Socialism can discourage inventions because no one will make a serious attempt in bringing a positive change through science and innovations as such attempts will not bring a major reward for the inventor.

g) **Socialism ignores morality** – It is condemned on ethical grounds too. Socialism is said that it is utilitarian, opportunistic, unduly materialistic, and devoid of any eternal law of truth and righteousness.

Charles Fourier

Karl Marx

Friedrich Engles

Political Philosophy: -
<u>Nehruvian Socialism</u>

Originally secularism as a political idea in the West, is commonly defined as the separation of the Church from civil affairs and the State, and may be broadened to a similar position seeking to remove or to minimise the role of religion in any public sphere. It may connote anti-clericalism, atheism, naturalism, non-sectarianism, neutrality on topics of religion or complete removal of religious symbols from public institutions.

Jawaharlal Nehru's Idea of Secularism: -

'Nehruvian Secularism' is a term used to describe philosophy of secularism propagated by India's first Prime Minister Pandit Jawaharlal Nehru. His philosophy sought to build a democratic, secular, and socialist India that respected diversity of its people, and is rooted in the idea of India as a pluralistic and diverse society, where individuals are free to practice their religion or religious belief without fear of persecution.

Origin: -

Nehruvian idea of secularism emerged in the years leading up to the independence of India in August, 1947. Our country has a long history of religious and cultural diversity, with many distinct communities living together for centuries. However, this unity was often undermined by the colonial administrators in line with their policy of 'divide and rule.' These colonialists frequently sought to impose English values and culture on the suppressed Indian masses.

Jawaharlal Nehru and other Indian independence leaders like *Maulana Azad, Babu Rajendra Prasad, Sardar Patel, Rafi Ahmed Kidwai,* etc recognised the importance of preserving India's diversity and promoting tolerance and respect for all religious, linguistic, and cultural groups. They strongly believed that this was essential and imperative for building a strong, prosperous, democratic nation.

Nehru's secular concept (unlike the western concept) was not concerned with the separation of 'Church and the State,' but was concentrated on promoting social and economic justice, human rights, and the welfare of all citizens regardless of their religion or belief system. Nehru propagated the idea that secularism was not just a political philosophy but a way of life that could help build a better and more peaceful world.

Characteristics: -

Nehruvian idea of secularism has several key features and characteristics that set it apart from other ideas and concepts.

First, it recognised the importance of religious and cultural diversity and sought to promote respect for all communities.

Second, it talks about promoting of social and economic justice. Pundit Nehru believed that the government had a responsibility to ensure that all citizens had access to basic needs such as education, housing, healthcare, and employment opportunities.

Third, Nehruvian secularism is deeply committed to human rights and welfare of all citizens. At the core this concept of secularism believes in the protection of the rights of the minorities and marginalised groups.

There has been a growing trend towards majoritarianism, where minority rights are often ignored in favour of the majority. This has led to the undermining of the principles of human rights and the welfare of all citizens that were central to Nehruvian secularism. It remains an important and relevant philosophy till date.

Pandit Jawaharlal Nehru

Nehru addressing a campaign rally. Secularism was one of the themes he stressed in a recently partitioned country.

Global Politics and International Relations: -

Feminist Perspective on IR

From the outset, feminist theory has challenged women's near complete absence from traditional International Relations theory and practice. This absence is visible both in women being marginalised from the ambit of decision making and in the assumption that the reality of women's lives is not impacted by or important to international relations. Beyond this, feminist contributions to every paradigm and domain of IR can be understood through their deconstruction of gender – both as socially constructed identities and as a powerful organising logic.

This means recognising and then challenging assumptions about masculine and feminine gender roles that dictate what both men and women should or can do in global politics and what counts as important in considerations of international relations. These assumptions in turn shape the process of global politics and the impact it has on the lives of ordinary men and women. Rather, it suggests that traditional IR theory was gender – neutral, i.e. it propagates, gender and IR are two separate spheres that did not impact on each other – feminist theory has shown that traditional IR is in fact gender – blind.

Feminist scholars therefore, takes both women and gender seriously and in doing so it challenges IR's foundational concepts and assumptions. Compared to other social sciences, feminist perspectives entered the discipline of international relations (IR) relatively late – at end of 1980's. Asking why IR remained immune to gender for so long, *Margot Light* has suggested that IR scholars have tended to view gender as an international problem, irrelevant to international relations.

It is not coincidental that feminist perspective entered the discipline at the same time as the end of the cold war and the consequent lessening in the predominance of military security issues that had tended to dominate IR since its founding. Previously obscured by East – West rivalry, a variety of issues, such as ethnic conflicts, economic globalisation, democratisation, and human rights began to occupy the IR agenda in the late 1980's. While international politics has never been just about relations between states, increasingly it has been defined in terms of relationships between international organisations and non-state actors such as transnational corporations, social movements, and international non-governmental organisations (NGOs).

This broad set of issues and a more comprehensive definition of global politics offered an entry point for feminist approaches. While women have always been player in international politics their voices have rarely been heard in the halls of state powers.

Feminist Theory: -

Feminists like *Sandra Whitworth* say that knowledge emerges from political practice, many feminists do believe in this notion. In 1990's, the introduction postmodern and post – colonial perspectives generated debate within feminist theory that had important implications for feminist perspective on IR.

Postmodernism has viewed with suspicion any mode of feminist thought that has tried to provide the feminist explanation as to why women are oppressed. Challenging arbitrary boundaries between reason and emotion, mind and body, feminist post-modernism has criticised the entire conceptual scheme of western dualistic thinking and its generated implications.

Feminists in IR have drawn from all these theoretical traditions. While there is an established liberal literature within feminist perspective of IR much of which focuses on foreign policy, opinion, to which many would identify themselves as post liberals in that they challenge the claim that women can simply be added to existing theoretical frameworks; they also acknowledge the centrality of gender as a category of analysis. Although many would deny the label, 'post – modern,' most have been influenced by postmodern and post-colonial approaches and their emphasis on difference among women.

Despite diversity of thought, debates in feminist perspective have been muted and there has not been a great deal of self – criticism among them. This maybe due in part to the relative newness of the approach; it may also be because despite its rapid growth, the feminist perspective is still quite marginalised. Since, their theoretical orientation is constantly struggling to be heard by wider discipline, they maybe reluctant to engage in self – criticism.

Nevertheless, in summarising some of the issues and questions with which feminists in IR have been concerned, here I will attempt to identify a few of these debates between them.

They have engaged a wide variety of international issues including security, global economy, development in the global south, human rights, global governance, a worldwide democratisation, and free maritime passage. In order to, illustrate some of the paths they have taken over the past ten years and some the emergent debates, I would like to draw the readers attention to three issues in particular – Development; Global Economy; and International Security. These three issues will in future be the most important and decisive on the international scale. For instance, on Development there is a constant friction between the west (United States in particular) and China. The communist nation's dreaded BRI Project (Belt & Road Initiative) is aimed at establishing its monopoly on most of the world trade and to basically colonise poor countries by offering loans with exponential interest rates, for example – Sri Lanka financial crisis of 2022, etc. China's *'debt trap diplomacy'* is unacceptable. This project is also a cause of concern for us (India) as a major part of this infrastructure project passes through the Pakistan occupied Kashmir (PoK) which is an integral part of the Indian Union.

In Global Economy, *BRICS* (Brazil, Russia, India, China, South Africa) has emerged as an important block banded together to form an alternated international currency to counter the influence of the United States Dollar (USD), and with the addition of Egypt, Ethiopia, Iran, and United Arab Emirates (UAE) in January, 2024 this effort of dethroning the USD as the sole global currency is gathering momentum.

International Security is the most discussed issue and the most important one too. With full – scale wars raging in the Middle – East, Ukraine, a raging civil war in Sudan between the Sudanese Armed Forces (SAF) and the Rapid Support Forces (RSF), the Sudanese paramilitary, and as it becomes more and more obvious that Donald Trump might return as the

US President this November a likelihood scenario of tensions flaring up between US and North Korea seems to be in the ambit of reality.

It is clear from the writings of professor *J. Ann. Tickner* that there are gendered perceptions in international relations, hidden by perpetrated 'gender neutrality' and 'objectivity.' In other words, although women and gender are both important parts of the daily operation and scholarship of IR, this presence is neither debated nor analysed by most theorists. In this way feminist perspective on IR challenges other strands and perspectives of IR on several levels, contributing to the major theoretical debates in the discipline and raising new areas of analysis.

Sandra Whitworth

J. Ann. Tickner

Global Politics and International Relations: -

Decolonisation in South East Asia.

Introducing the concept of colonialism and de-colonialism. Examine the anti-colonial struggles in context of Asian countries: -

Colonialism is a practice or policy of control by one people or power over other people or areas, often by establishing and generally with the aim of economic dominance. In the process of colonisation, colonisers may impose their religion, language, economics, and other cultural practices. The foreign administrators rule the territory in pursuit of their interests, seeking to benefit from the colonised region's people and resources. It is associated with but distinct from imperialism.

Colonialism is a practice of domination, which involves the subjugation of one people to another. Oneof the difficulties in defining colonialism is that it is hard to distinguish it from imperialism. Frequently the two concepts are treated as synonyms. Like colonialism, imperialism also involves political and economic control over a dependent territory. The etymology of the two terms, however, provides some clues about how they differ. The term colony comes from the Latin word *colonus*, meaning farmer. This root reminds us that the practice of colonialism usually involved the transfer of population to a new territory, where the arrivals lived as permanent settlers while maintaining political allegiance to their country of origin. Imperialism, on the other hand, comes from the Latin term *imperium*, meaning to command. Thus, the term imperialism draws attention to the way that one country exercises power over another, whether through settlement, sovereignty, or indirect mechanisms of control.

The legitimacy of colonialism has been a longstanding concern for political and moral philosophers inthe Western tradition. At least since the Crusades and the conquest of the Americas, political theorists have struggled with the difficulty of reconciling ideas about justice and natural law with the practice of European sovereignty over non-Western peoples. In the nineteenth century, the tension between liberal thought and colonial practice became particularly acute, as dominion of Europe over the rest of the worldreached its zenith. Ironically, in the same period when most political philosophers began to defend the principles of universalism and equality, the same individuals still defended the legitimacy of colonialism and imperialism. One way of reconciling those apparently opposed principles was the argument known asthe "civilizing mission," which suggested that a temporary period of political dependence or tutelage was necessary for "uncivilized" societies to advance to the point where they were capable of sustaining liberal institutions and self-government.

Most of the colonies were owned by European powers: -

a) Britain's Empire was the largest in area, consisting of *India, Burma, Ceylon, Malaya,* enormous tracts of *Africa* including *Egypt* and *Sudan,* and many assorted islands and other territories such as Cyprus, Hong Kong, the West Indies, the Falkland Islands and Gibraltar.

b) France had second largest empire, with territories in Africa, Indo-China.

c) In addition, Britain, and France both held territories in the *Middle-East,* taken from Turkey at the end of the First World War. Britain controlled *Transjordan* and *Palestine* and France held *Syria.*

d) Other important empires were those of the

Netherlands (Dutch East Indies), Belgium (Congo and Ruanda-Urundi), Portugal (Angola, Mozambique, and Guinea), Spain (Spanish Sahara, Ifni, Spanish Morocco and Spanish Guinea and Italy (Libya, Somalia, and Eritrea).

Over the next 30 years after the Second World War ended in 1945, remarkable changes took place. By 1975 the process of decolonisation (as it will be known later) was almost complete. Sometimes, the struggles for independence and self-determination were hard fought. **decolonisation** is the undoing of colonialism, the latter being the process whereby a nation establishes and maintains its domination of foreign territories. The concept particularly applies to the dismantlement,during the second half of the 20th century, of the colonial empires established prior to the First World War throughout the world. Some scholars of decolonization focus especially on the movements in the colonies demanding independence.

Decolonization may involve either nonviolent revolution or national liberation wars by pro-independencegroups. It may be international or involve the intervention of foreign powers acting individually or through international bodies such as the United Nations. These include the breakup of the Spanish Empire in the 19th century; of the German, *Austro-Hungarian* and *Russian empires* following the First World War of the *British, French, Dutch, Portuguese, Belgian, Italian*, and *Japanese* colonial empires following the Second World War; and of the Soviet Union at the end of the Cold War.

Decolonization has been used to refer to the intellectual decolonization from the colonizer's ideas that made the colonized feel inferior. Issues of decolonization persist and are raised contemporarily.

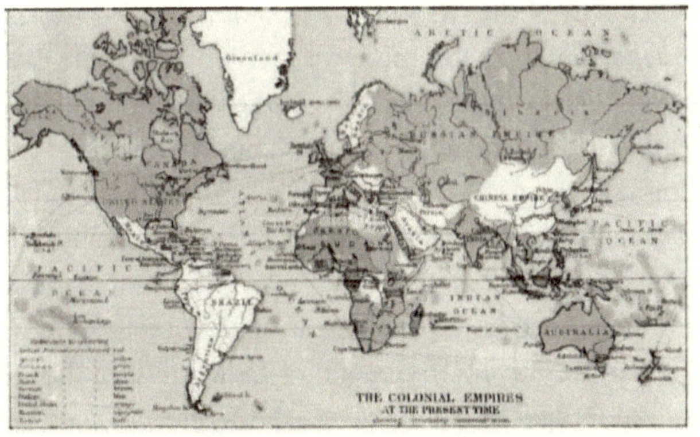

A map of Colonial Empires around the world.

<u>Case studies of anti-colonial struggles in some Asian countries:-</u>

India: -

In *India* anti-colonial struggle began in 1850's, which lead to the *'Revolt of 1857'* or the *'First War of Independence'*. After the great revolt of 1857, the nationalist sentiment began to surge which gradually lead to the organization of the Indian National Conference in 1884, and a year later the Indian National Congress was born. Congress lead many struggles against the British, however it became much more involved in the freedom struggle after *Lord Curzon* the Governor-General of India, divided the stateof Bengal into two halves, the West Bengal comprising of a Hindu majority with Calcutta as its capital and East Bengal comprising of a Muslim majority with Murshidabad as its capital. The early leaders of the Congress like *Sri Aurobindo Ghosh, Bal Gangadhar Tilak, Lala Lajpat Rai, Bipin Chandra Pal,* etc.; saw this attempt as a practice of the policy of *'divide and rule.'* Their fierce opposition led to the annulment of the partition of Bengal in December, 1911.

The arrival of *Mahatma Gandhi* in India in 1915 completely re-energised the Congress and the freedom movement. Gandhiji brought in young leaders like

Pundit Jawaharlal Nehru, Sardar Patel, Dr.Rajendra Prasad, etc. Congress under Gandhiji launched various movements like Non-cooperation movement (1920-1922); Civil-Disobedience movement (1930); Quit India Movement (1942). These peaceful yet phenomenal movements made the British rulers weak and terrified. As the mighty British Empire was battered after the Second World War, the Congress was successful in getting the independence from the British rule in August, 1947.

French Indo-China: -

The people of *Indo-China* were fighting the French rule for gaining their independence and self-determination for a very long period. Indo-China remained under the French occupation for over a hundred years. However, these struggles weren't organised and carefully orchestrated and that is why these struggles were not long lasting. After Ho Chi Minh formed the Communist Party of Indo-China, all the anti-colonial forces including the nationalists came on a single platform.

After the World War, France petitioned for the nullification of the 1938 Franco-Siamese Treaty and reasserted itself in the region, but came into conflict with the *Viet Minh*, a coalition of Communists and Vietnamese nationalists led by *Ho Chi Minh*, founder of the Indochinese Communist Party. During World War II, the United States had supported the Viet Minh in resistance against the Japanese; the group had been in control of the countryside since the French gave way in March 1945.

However, 1950 was the turning point of the war. Ho's government was recognised by the fellow Communist governments of China and the Soviet Union, and Mao's government subsequently gave a fallback position to Ho's forces, as well as abundant supplies of weapons. In October 1950, the French army suffered its first major defeat with the battle of Route Coloniale 4, also called the Autumn-Winter Border Campaign. Subsequent efforts by the French military managed to improve their situation only in the short term. *Bao Dại's* State of Vietnam proved a weak and unstable government, and *Norodom Sihanouk's* Cambodia proclaimed its independence in November 1953. Fighting lasted until May 1954, when the *Viet Minh* won the decisive victory against French forces at the grueling battle of *Dien Bien Phu*. After the Geneva Agreements the Indo-China gained its independence but was divided into three parts, Vietnam, Laos, and Cambodia.

An artist's depiction of the Battle of Plassey (1757). It is termed as the most crucial battel in terms of its imperativeness, as it paved the way for the establishment of British Suzerainty over India.

It was fought between the forces of the Nawab of Bengal, Siraj-ud-Daula and East India Company forces under Robert Clive.

A portrait of Lord Dalhousie. Through his policies of Subsidiary Alliance; Doctrine of Lapse; and false pretext Maladministration he orchestrated the biggest land grab in India by taking away entire kingdoms from Indian Princes.

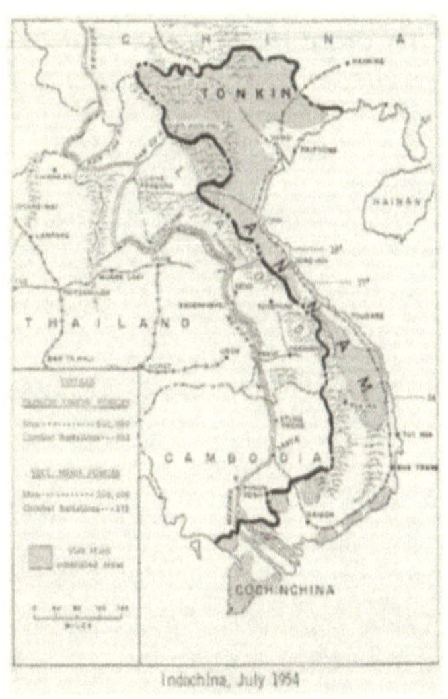

A map of Frech Indo-China from mid-Twentieth Century.

A picture of Ho Chi Minh, the leader of Viet Minh and later President of Democratic Republic of Vietnam (North-Vietnam).

This page intentionally blank.

Global Politics and International Relations: -

China's Rise

"Let China sleep. For when she wakes, the world will tremble"

-Napoleon Bonaparte

(Emperor of the French)

China, now the second most populous country in the world, has experienced a significant economic growth in the recent decades. This has resulted in China becoming a global economic superpower in every sense, with a positive trade surplus. However, many experts of South-East Asia affairs have speculated for long that China is using its economic relationships and trade surplus to build military power in Asia and beyond. India, as China's neighbour is particularly concerned with this development.

China's Economic Relations and Positive Trade Surplus: -

China has, over many decades developed relationships with many countries around the world, particularly in Asia and Africa. China's trade surplus, which refers to the amount by which its exports exceed its imports has been steadily increasing since 1980's. In 2020 itself, China's trade surplus amounted to approximately $535 billion (USD). This has allowed China to invest heavily in building its military prowess, particularly in the Naval and Air wings of the People's Liberation Army (PLA).

In addition to this trade surplus, China has also invested in magnanimous infrastructure projects around the world through its Belt and Road Initiative Programme (BRI) which involves China spending over a trillion dollars on infrastructure projects, like – roads, railways, ports, airports, etc. in more than 60 countries. It is the flagship project of the Chinese government under Xi Jinping and is aimed at reviving the old 'silk road' and the promote economic development and trade, but it has been rightly criticised for allowing China to phenomenally increase its presence and influence in other countries.

Impact of China's Economic Rise on India: -

China's economic rise and its trade relations have had a significant impact on India's military power status. India has long been concerned about China's rise in economic and military power development and its growing influence in the region. China's investments in infrastructure projects in India's neighbours such as, Pakistan and Sri Lanka, have given China a strategic advantage in the region.

China's naval and air forces have also become significantly powerful, which has raised concerns in India has responded by increasing its own military spending and investing in its naval and air forces. As of February, 2023 India has two aircraft carriers (INS Vikrant & INS Viraat) and an entire squadron of French made Rafael Jets.

China has also invested significantly in the development of Gwadar Seaport located in Baluchistan province of Pakistan. The development of this port has given China a strategic advantage in the region and raised concerns in India about China's intentions. India has responded by increasing its own investment in the development of the Chabahar Port in Iran, which is intended to provide India with an alternative trade route to Afghanistan, Central Asia, and West Asia. The recently announced International North-South Transport Corridor (INSTC) a multimode network of ports, roads, railways, etc extending between India, Iran, Azerbaijan, and Russia, beginning from Mumbai (India) and ending in Moscow (Russia), also aims at lessening China's influence in the region.

China's economic rise and it becoming a manufacturing hub has also impacted India's domestic economy. China's low-cost manufacturing has resulted in the flooding of India markets with cheap goods, which has hurt Indian industries. India has responded by implementing protection policies, such as increasing tariffs on Chinese goods.

In conclusion, I would like to say that China's stupendous economic growth has had significant on India and the world at large. It has also impacted India militarily. In response to its expansionist agenda, India has acted swiftly by exponentially increasing its defence spending. India has also sternly criticised the BRI programme as a stretch of it passes through Pakistan occupied Kasmir (PoK), an integral part of the Indian Union.

In recent years India has also joined security alliances and groups, like – Quadrilateral Alliance or QUAD, consisting of USA, India, Australia, and Japan. It was formed to check China's growing influence in the South-China Sea and for ensuring free maritime passage of goods from all countries. The relationship between India and China is complex to say the least and will continue to be so for the foreseeable future. India and China started diplomatic relations in 1950 and India became the first non-socialist state to recognise the People's Republic of China and established diplomatic relations. The infamous slogan, *Hindi-Chini Bhai Bhai* (Indians and

Chinese are Brothers) emerged during this period itself. Chinese Premier Zhou Enlai visited India in 1954. India and China put a joint statement and endorsed the Five Principles of *'Panchsheel.'* In the same year, Prime Minister Pandit Jawaharlal Nehru toured China. He was the first head of the government of a major state to visit, since the establishment of the People's Republic of China. In 1955, India and China participated in *Asian-African Conference* held in Indonesia and promoted the *Bandung Spirit* of friendship, unity, and cooperation. The Non- Aligned Movement was the result of this conference and in Belgrade, Yugoslavia, the first NAM summit took place in 1961. Nehru saw China as the potential partner in the Asian region. However, the Sino-India war of 1962 resulted in major setbacks in bilateral ties. The border war intensified India-China rivalry. Later developments such as the acquisition of nuclear weapons by China in 1964 and India's role in creation of Bangladesh as well as its nuclear weapons test in 1974 (Pokhran-I*), Nathu-La and Cho-La clashes of 1967*, further strained the India-China relationship.

The period between in 1980's and 1990's did see a normalisation of ties from both sides. Leaders from both countries visited each other, for instance – *Prime Minister Rajiv Gandhi* toured China in 1988; In 1992, *R. Venkatraman* became the first Indian President to visit China since 1947; *Chinese President Jiang Zemin's* trip to India in 1996 was the first visit by a Chinese President; *Prime Minister P. V. Narasimha*

Rao visited China in 1993 and signed the Maintenance of Peace and Tranquillity along the Line of Actual Control (LAC) along India-China border. Relations were on an upward trend in the 21st century too. Chinese President, *Xi Jinping* visited India thrice, since 2014. *Prime Minister Narendra Modi* has also visited China five times in his tenure.

However, the deadly *Galwan Valley* clashes of 2020 between India and China, which tragically left 20 Indian soldiers dead and an unknown number of Chinese soldiers too, has greatly soured the relations between the two. Since the 2020 clash, China has aggressively pursued to its expansionist policies, 'Salamy Slicing' the territories of Bhutan, renaming of the cities in Arunachal Pradesh. Such actions show a confrontational pattern and are extremely dangerous for world peace.

***India shares a 3488 km long border with China. This border is disputed in three sectors: -**

1) **The Western Sector: -**
India shares a length of approximately 2152 kms with China's border in western sector,which covers an area between *Jammu and Kashmir* and China's *Xinjiang* Province. In western sector, the dispute is for the Aksai Chin region of Jammu and Kashmir (till 2019 and part of Union Territory of Ladakh, 2019 onwards). The British Empire was

responsible for the dispute over the Aksai Chin region. It is due to their failure to draw a clear and legitimate border between India and China. *Two borders - the Johnson Line* and *the Macdonald Line* were recommended between India and China during the British Empire. According to Johnson Line Aksai Chin falls under Indian territory. According to the Macdonald Line, Aksai China falls under Chinese territory. India contemplates Johnson Line as the accurate line and the legal national boundary with China. Similarly, China appraisesthe Macdonald Line as the right border with India. A line that separates Indian administered areas of Jammu and Kashmir from Aksai Chin is called the Line of Actual Control (LAC). India and China fought a war in 1962 over disputed territory of Aksai Chin. India asserts that Aksai Chin is an integral part of the Union Territory of Ladakh, while China declares that it was a part of Xinjiang province.

2) **The Middle Sector: -**

India shares a length of 625 kms with China in the middle sector, which runs along the border with *Ladakh, Himachal Pradesh, Uttarakhand* then onto Nepal. This sector is completely dispute free, in respect of the border. The only conflict seen in this sector was in Sikkim. In 2003, during the visit of Prime Minister Shri Atal Bihari Vajpayee, China recognised India's sovereignty over Sikkim. India-China opened *Nathu La Pass* for cross border trade. Nepal

3) **The Eastern Sector: -**

India shares a length of 1149 kms of land boundary with China, starting from Bhutan'seastern point to a point close to the *Talu Pass* at the trijunction of *Tibet, Myanmar*, and India. This line is known as the *McMahon Line* named after *Henry McMahon,* a representative of the British Government who signed the *Shimla Convention (1913-14)*. China claimed, McMahon Line was illegal and unacceptable. They further reiterated their claim that Tibet has no legitimate right to sign the Shimla Convention, as it was an imperial boundary and claiming *Tawang* region of Arunachal Pradesh as an extension of Tibet, hence part of Chinese territory. The British accepted Chinese sovereignty over Tibet. However, they divided it into two parts: Inner Tibet – full sovereignty of China and Outer Tibet – *Tawang* region in the Indian State of Arunachal Pradesh. This region is fully under the control of Government of India.

Mao Zedong, leader of the Communist Party of China, declaring the establishment of People's Republic of China, in 1949.

Leaders of the two Asian Giants meet.

Prime Minister Nehru with Chairman Mao Zedong, 1954.

Chinese Premier Zhou Enlai meets Prime Minister Nehru, April 1960.

Prime Minister Narendra Modi greeting Chinese President Xi Jinping.

This meeting took place when President Xi visited the South Indian city of Chennai for India-China Summit, October, 2019.

Galwan Valley: China and India clash on freezing and inhospitable battlefield

2020 Galwan Valley clashes between the two Asian giants was the deadliest since 1967.

QUAD Summit, Sydney 2023.

(L-R) Prime Minister of Australia, Anthony Albanese;

President of the United States, Joseph. R. Biden;
Prime Minister of India, Narendra Modi;

and Prime Minister of Japan, Fumio Kishida.

Global Politics and International Relations: - <u>World-Systems Theory</u>

The *World-Systems theory* also known as system analysis is a multidisciplinary approach to world history and social change which emphasises the world system as the primary unit of social analysis. It refers to the inter-regional and transnational division of labour, which divides the world into *core countries*, *semi-periphery* countries. Core-countries focus on higher skills, capital-intensive production, and the rest of the world focuses on low-skill, labour-intensive production, and extraction of and extraction of raw materials.

This structure is unified by the division of labour. It is a world economy rooted in a capitalist system, for a particular time, certain countries become hegemon. In the past few decades, this status has passed from *Netherlands* to the *United Kingdom*, and finally to the *United States*.

World-Systems theory has attracted criticisms from its rivals, notably for being too focused on economy and not enough on culture and being too core-centric and state-centric.

William I. Robinson* has criticized the World-Systems theory for its nation-state centrism, state-structural approach, and its inability to conceptualized the rise of globalization. Robinson suggests, that world system theory does not account for emerging transnational social force and the relationships forged between them and global institutions serving their interests. These forces operate on a global rather than state system and cannot be understood be understood by *Wallerstein's* nation-centred approach.

According to Wallerstein himself, critique of the world system approach comes from four directions, the positivists, the orthodox Marxists, the autonomists and the culturalists.

The Positivist Critique: -

They criticise the theory because according to them it is too prone to generalisation, lacking qualitative data and failing to put forth a falsifiable proposition.

Marxist Critique: -

Orthodox Marxists find the world systems theory deviating too far from orthodox Marxist principles, such as by not giving enough weight to the concept of social class.

Autonomist Critique: -

The Autonomists criticise the world-systems theory for blurring the boundaries between state and business. Further, positivists and autonomists argue that the state should be the central unit of analysis.

Cultural Critique: -

The culturalists argue that the world systems theory puts too much importance on the economy and not enough on the culture.

William I. Robinson

Immanuel Wallerstein

Global Politics and International Relations: -

<u>Treaty of Westphalia</u>

The Treaty of Westphalia is the collective name for two peace treaties signed in the October of 1648 in the *Westphalian* cities of *Osnabruck* and *Munster*. The signing of this treaty ended the Thirty-Year War and brought peace to the *Holy Roman Empire* closing calamitous period in the history of Europe, that killed approximately eight million people (soldiers and peasants).

The Holy Roman Emperor, King of Spain, Kingdoms of France and Sweden, The United Provinces of Netherlands, and their respective allies among the princes of the Holy Roman Empire, participated in these treaties.

Negotiations were lengthy and complex. Talks took place in two cities because each side wanted to meet on the territory under its control. Almost 109 delegations arrived to represent the belligerent states. Tow treaties signed at Munster and Osnabruck ended the Thirty-Year War in the Holy Roman Empire, with the Hapsburgs and their Catholic allies on one side and the Protestant powers on the other.

Scholars of International Relations have identified the Peace of Westphalia as the origin of the principles, crucial to modern perspectives on International Relations, collectively known as Westphalian Sovereignty, though others argue that this is largely a myth invented by the fact, that – Europe had been battered by the Thirty-Year War and the Eighty-Year War (between Spain and United Provinces), exacting a heavy toll on money and lives. The Eighty-Year War was a prolonged struggle for the independence of Netherlands, and was supported by England against Spain, and Portugal. It was a partly religious and partly and mostly dynastic power struggle. The War included a large number of players, siding either with the House of Hapsburg or the House of Bourbon, the factionalism was more complex than mere dynastic allegiances.

With between 4.5 million and 8 million dead in the Thirty-Years War alone, and warfare, the need for peace became increasingly clear.

The Contributions of the Treaty of Westphalia: -

1) The power asserted by the Holy Roman Emperor was stripped and returned to the rulers of imperial states. Hence, it ended the Catholic and Protestant rivalry, bringing peace.

2) Catholics and Protestants were redefined as
   equal before the law.
3) The independents of the Dutch Republic saw
   it become a safe haven for Jews.
4) Barriers to trade and commerce erected
   during the war were abolished.
5) For the first time in History major European
   powers came together on a single table to end
   violence and bloodshed.
6) The signing of the treaty showed that violence
   and war are not the only solution to political
   problems. This treaty showed the world that
   war could be supplanted by diplomacy.

A portrait depicting the signing of Treaty of Westphalia.

Global Politics and International Relations: -
<u>End of Cold War</u>

The world had entered the post-Cold War era in 1992. Many efforts were made since the 1950's to promote relaxing of tension and on many occasions in the past it appeared that the two power blocks had entered the period of *'Detente'*. Gradually however, the cold war came to an end. This was due to the operation of several factors acting in tandem.

1) One of the most important factors that played an increasingly important role in changing the policy of confrontation was the realisation that unlike at any time before in human history, the predictability of all out was simply could not the basis of conducting international relations.

2) The reports prepared by the scientists on the effects of a nuclear war and the voices raised by them against the armaments race and the doctrine of *'Mutually Assured Destruction'* and Nuclear Deterrence and the popular movements in every art of the world played an important role in creating an atmosphere of 'Detente.'

3) Further, since the 1960's the rigid alliances showed tendency of breaking down. From 1954

onward, Soviet leaders began laying stress on peaceful co-existence, after the split in the communist movement in the late 1950's. The theory of *'Dangers from the Expansion of Communism'* lost much of its relevance. Hostilities between the Soviet Union, and China destroyed the fear of communism which had earlier been viewed as a monolith bloc.

4) The policies pursued by *Mikail Gorbachev* who came to power in 1985 were also a seminal development that finally brought the Cold War to an end.

5) The factors like weak Soviet Economy after the defeat in the Afghan War had a huge role in the Soviet Union.

6) Gorbachev's policies of *'Glasnost'* (openness) and *'Perestroika'* (restructuring) lead to the weakening of Moscow's control over the Soviet satellite states, for example – reunification of Germany in 1989; formation of an anti-communist solidarity government in Poland.

End of Cold War: -

The cold war got virtually ended when the liberalisation and democratisation of Eastern European countries took place when the Berlin wall was demolished and Germany unified; Warsaw Pact was liquidated, and when erstwhile adversaries east and west got engaged in a process of peaceful co-existence and mutual co-operation for development.

Rise of Unipolarity in International Relations: -

The Bi-polarity of 1950's was replaced by unipolarity in 1990's. The end of the Cold War did not return the world to multipolarity. Instead, the United States – already materially preeminent – became more so. We currently live in a one superpower world, a circumstance unprecedented in the modern era. No other great power has enjoyed such advantages in material capabilities – military, economic, technological, and geographical. Other states rival the United States in one area or another, but the multifaceted character of American power places it in a category of its own. The collapse of the Soviet Union and its empire, slower economic growth in Japan and Western Europe during the 1990s, and America's outsized military spending have all enhanced these disparities. While in most historical eras the distribution of capabilities among major states has tended to be multipolar or bipolar – with several major states of roughly equal size and capability – the United States emerged from the 1990s as an unrivalled global power.

Changes in the Polics of Europe: -

The collapse of communist bloc and the USSR (Soviet Union) was accompanied by the end of Russian role in European politics. The rise of non-communist regimes through movements for democracy and liberalisation in the eastern European States gave a new look to European politics.

Changes in Asian Politics: -

Under the impact of the collapse of the Soviet Union. Politics in Asia underwent a big change. In particular, India lost one of its best, time-tested and dependable allies. After the collapse of the USSR, another Asian power, China also felt isolated as a communist state.

Rise of several Economic Blocs: -

After the collapse of the socialist bloc International economic system began undergoing big changes. APEC; AFTA; NAFTA; PIF; SCO; G7; G20, besides – EU; ASEAN; SAARC, OPEC got engaged in active economic diplomacy and cooperation in IR.

Thus, collapse of USSR along with the end of Cold-War, liberalisation of eastern Europe, and emergence of unipolar world in power structure and ideological environment acted as a source of profound and big changes in IR of the last decade of 20th century.

German people celebrate the reunification of Germany at the Brandenburg Gate, 1989.

Mikail Gorbachev, last leader of the Soviet Union.

His policies of 'Glasnost' and 'Perestroika' paved the way for the collapse of USSR.

After the collapse of Soviet Union India moved rapidly towards liberalisation of its economy. Then Finance Minister, Dr. Manmohan Singh is considered to the chief architect of the Liberalisation, Privatisation, Globalisation or LPG reforms.

Governance and Policy Making: -

<u>Land Reforms & Green Revolution</u>

Land reforms and the Green Revolution have been two of the most significant development in post-independence India. These have had a major impact on our country's agricultural sector and have helped to spur economic growth and reduce poverty. Let us discuss and examine the nature and impact of these reforms, and discuss the challenges they faced and continue to face.

Land Reforms in India: -

They are a set of measures aimed at improving the ownership and distribution of Land, particularly in the rural areas. In India, the union government has implemented several land reforms since independence, with the primary aim of improving the livelihoods of small and marginal farmers and reducing poverty and inequalities.

One of the key reforms introduced was the *Zamindari Abolition Act (1950).* Zamindari were the intermediaries, controlling large amounts of land but did not work it themselves. These reforms helped plenty in reducing the concentration of land ownership and transfer control of the land to those who worked it. Government of India also introduced reforms aimed at ensuring fair and equal access to land, for example – distribution of surplus land to landless and small farmers. Government also brought in policies for the amelioration of the farmers and their recently acquired land, for example – recognition of their rights to ownership and the introduction of Land records. Despite these reforms, land ownership and distribution in India remains highly unequal, and a large proportion of the rural population continues to be landless or has limited access to land. The implementation of land reforms has been slow and uneven, measured introduced have been limited. Lack of effective enforcement mechanisms has meant systemic failure.

Green Revolution in India: -

The green or agrarian revolution was a series of technological, institutional, and scientific changes that that transformed the agricultural sector in India in the 1960's – 1970's. Green Revolution was characterised by the adoption of new high-yielding varieties of seeds, the increased use of fertilisers and irrigation, and the expansion of credit and marketing facilities for farmers.

It had a tremendous impact on the agricultural sector in India, leading to significant increases food production and agricultural productivity. India was able to achieve self – sufficiency in food grain production, the growth of agrarian sector helped to reduce poverty and spur economic growth. It also helped to increase the incomes of farmers particularly small and marginal ones.

However, this large scale and instant adoption of modern farming practices did not come without challenges and drawbacks. The widespread adoption of new technology, usage of fertilisers and pesticides resulted in the increased costs for farmers.

Land Reforms along with the Green Revolution have been two of the most significant developments in post – independence India. Nevertheless, these reforms have faced significant developments in post-independence India including resistance from powerful land owners.

Dr. M. S. Swaminathan, the father of India's Green Revolution. His attempts for making India self-reliant in food production is commendable.

Prime Minister Mrs. Indira Gandhi is widely credited with commencing the program of Green Revolution.

Governance and Policy Making: -

Changing nature of Indian Party System

Many scholars believe, Indian Party System is unique in every sense of the word. It does not fit in any kind classification that is generally used to categorise the party systems. It is defined by the singular nature of Indian politics on the one hand and the nature of the state-society relationship on the other.

In the last two decades there has been substantial change both in politics as well as in nature of relationship between the state and the society.

One of the various important manifestations of change is visible in the context of the politicisation of greater number of people, especially those belonging to the less privileged sections of society. That explains the change of the party systems as well. The distinctive features that defined the party system of India in the first two decades after independence are no more to be seen at present.

India's party system evolves from an identifiable political centre. This political centre, carved during the nationalist movement, was comprised of the political elite sharing common social background.

1) **Dominant Party System (1947-67) –** Dominance of the Congress Party it was known to be the central institution of Indian politics. Congress's centrality was reflected at following levels.

   (a) At one level, it occupied the most central space of electoral politics. It monopolised the situation by not allowing other parties to seriously challenge its position.

   (b) Congress's centrality was reflected in its ideology. Congress has been an umbrella party having space for all ideological groups.

2) **Dislocation of Political Centre –** The emergence of the new political classes was directly related to the rise of the propriety peasant class in rural India in the backdrop of the land reforms. These new political classes dislocated the Congress from its position of centrality. The formation of the Bahujan Samaj Party (BSP), Samajwadi Party (SP), Janta Dal are examples of these new political classes forming their political movements.

3) **Emergence of more regional/caste-based parties –** After the fourth general election led to the beginning of the politics of coalition.

This election produced truncated majority of the Congress, coalitions emerged in many states with Jana Sangh, CPI, CPM, etc at the helm.

At the centre too various opposition parties stitched a grand opposition coalition called the 'Janata Party.' During this phrase (1967-77) framework began to crumble.

4) **Loss of Centrality of the Congress** – This period commenced in 1989. After the general elections Congress was displaced from its position of centrality.

Following factors are responsible to this: -

a) Congress was no longer the dominant political party. There were several regional players like the Bhartiya Janata Party (BJP), Bahujan Samaj Party (BSP), Dravida Munnetra Kazhagam (DMK), etc, in sight.

b) Failure of the Congress to garner most votes enabled regional parties to gain ground. That is the main reason why large parties like the Congress and the BJP depended on the regional parties from 1989-2014.

c) **Contemporary Party System** – The vacuum created by the Congress's decimation has been filled by the BJP and regional parties. This period (2014-Present) has seen a reversal from the era of one-party dominance. In this case the BJP has emerged victorious in two consecutive general elections (2014&2019), winning as much as 303 seats in the Lok Sabha in 2019, twice forming a one-party majority government at the centre. In 2024 General Elections however, the opposition INDIA (Indian National Developmental Inclusive Alliance) trounced the BJP to reach a whopping 237 seats in the Lok Sabha, coercing the BJP to form a *minority government* with the support of Janata Dal United (JDU) and Telugu Desam Party (TDP). This boost for the opposition alliance mainly came from the states of Uttar Pradesh, West Bengal and Maharashtra.

The current system is defined by its multiplicity. Several national and regional parties have filled in the vacuum created by the Congress' s decimation from its central position. This has strengthened India's federal structure.

NOTE

This essay was written before the general elections, but the outcome of the polls on June 4th, 2024, brought about substantial changes. In light of these developments, I have edited and refined this piece to ensure its relevance and accuracy."

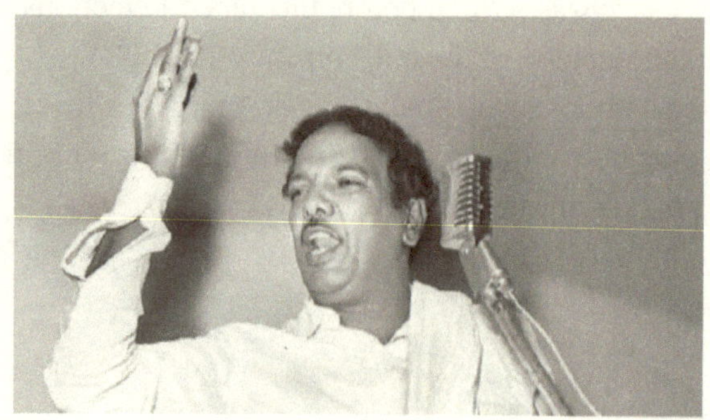

*M. Karunanidhi was the founder of the DMK Party,
former Chief Minister of Tamil Nadu, and a leader in
Dravidian Politics.*

*Kanshiram was the founder of BSP, and a leading
voice of the Dalits and oppressed classes.*

INDIA Bloc Rally in Mumbai, March, 2024.

In the General Elections of 2024, the alliance secured 237 seats, coercing the BJP to lead a minority government.

(L-R) Prime Minister Modi, TDP leader and Andhra Pradesh Chief Minister N. Chandrababu Naidu,

and Bihar Chief Minister Nitish Kumar from the JDU. Mr Naidu and Mr Kumar are both crucial for the NDA government's survival.

First sitting of the 18th Lok Sabha.

Results of the General Elections produced an evenly divided Lok Sabha with a bolstered Opposition.

Governance and Policy Making: -

<u>Powers and Functions of MP's</u>

Members from both the houses of Parliament (Lok Sabha & Rajya Sabha) are the representatives of the people. The first instance of member of the Parliament equivalents in India dates to 9th December, 1946, the day Constituent Assembly of India first met.

The 1951-52 general elections brought in first set of Members of Parliament or MPs. Articles 79-122 in Part-V of the Constitution deals with the organisation, composition, duration, officers, procedures, privileges, powers, etc. The President of the Indian Union is not the member of either house of the Parliament. This is because a bill passed by both the Houses of Parliament, cannot become a law without the President's assent. In this respect Indian Constitution relies on the British pattern rather than American Pattern.

Powers of Members of Parliament: -

1) **Organs of Information** – MPs are referred to as, the 'Organs of Information.' Members of both Houses of Parliament constantly check

the powers of the government, they force the government to debate and discuss its policies.

2) Members of Parliament are guardians of privileges as they guard the privileges and rights of and ordinary citizen.

3) **Holding the Government to Account** – Members of Parliament hold the government to account. They question the Union Cabinet and even the Prime Minister.

4) **Control of Finances** – Members of the Parliament control the finances of the country. No tax can be spent without the consent of Parliamentarians.

Functions of Members of Parliament: -

1) **Legislative Functions** – The primary function of Members of Parliament is to make laws for the governance of the country. It has exclusive powers to make laws on the subjects enumerated in the Union list and concurrent list.

2) **Oversight Function** – Members of Parliament should ensure that the executive performs its duties.

3) **Representation of the People** – It is a duty and the function of an MP (Member of Parliament) to represent the views as aspirations of the people of their constituency in the Parliament.

4) **Amendment of the Constitution** – Parliament is vested with powers and functions to amend the constitution. Members of Parliament have the authority to amend the constitution under Article 368 of Part XX (20) of the Constitution.

5) **Judicial Functions** –

Members of Parliament have following judicial functions: -
a) The can, by passing an article of impeachment, impeach the President of the Indian Union from his office.
b) MPs can remove the Vice-President of India from his office.
c) They have the power and authority to impeach the Chief Justice of India and other Judges.

Member of Parliament Local Area Development Scheme (MPLAD)

It is a scheme formulated by the government of India on 23rd December, 1993. It enables the Member of Parliament to recommend developmental work in their constituencies with an emphasis on creating durable community assets based on locally felt needs.

This scheme was administered by Ministry of Rural Development. However, since October 1994 Ministry of Statistics and Programme Implementation. The driving idea behind this scheme is, a sum of money is given to each Member of Parliament for the development of his/her constituency. MPs are advised to work on key priorities – *safe drinking water facilities, non-conventional energy resources, healthcare and sanitation, irrigation facilities, railways, roads, bridges, etc.*

The Ministry of Statistics and Programme Implementation (MOSPI) has issued following guidelines for the scheme: -

1) Developmental projects implemented by the government agencies would now be provided 75% of the project cost in the first instalments.

2) In smaller projects costing less than 2 lakh
    rupees, the entire amount would be released at
    one go.

Nevertheless, such a scheme is bound to have flaws.
Its critical analysis is as follows: -

There are many issues with the MPLAD scheme.
Many say it breaches India's Federal structure. Union
Government can incur expenditure only with respect
to matters over which it has subject domain as per
seventh schedule. It encroaches upon the domain of
local self-governing institutions and thereby violates
Part IX (9) and IX-A (9-A) of the constitution.

This scheme conflicts with the *'doctrine of
separation of powers'* by involving MPs in executive
functions. Of course, there have been many
implementation lapses. The Comptroller and Auditor
General (CAG) has flagged instances of financial
mismanagement and malfeasance and artificial
inflation of amount of money spent.

It has no statutory backing i.e. it is not governed by
any statutory law and is under threat from the
government. In spite of all these flaws, issues,
criticisms, lapses; the MPLAD scheme continues to
serve the people of India.

Governance and Policy Making: -

<u>Right to Information Act</u>

Right to Information Act, 2005 mandates timely response to citizen requests for government information. It is an initiative taken by Department of Personnel and Training, Ministry of Personnel, Public Grievances and Pensions. The basic object of the Right to Information Act is to empower the citizens, promote transparency and accountability in the working of the government, contain corruption and make our democracy work for the people in real sense. It goes without saying that an informed citizen is better equipped to keep the necessary vigil on the instruments of governance and make the government more accountable to the governed. The Act is a big step towards making the citizens informed about activities of the government.

The Right to Information is an act passed by the parliament of India which sets out the rules and regarding citizen's right to information. It replaced the former Freedom of Information Act, 2002. Under the provisions of RTI Act, any citizen of India may request information from a "public authority" (a body of government or "instrumentality of State") which is required to reply expeditiously or within thirty days. In case of matter involving a petitioner's life and liberty, the information must be provided within fourty-eight hours. The Act also requires every public authority to computerised their records for wide dissemination and to proactively publish certain categories of information so that the citizens need minimum recourse to request for information formally.

The RTI Act was passed by the Parliament of India on 15th June 2005, and came into force with effect from 12th October, 2005. Every day on an average, over fourty-eight hundred RTI applications are filed. In first ten years of the commencement of the act over 17,500,000 applications had been filed.

Although, Right to Information is not included as a fundamental right in the Constitution of India, it protects the fundamental rights to Freedom of Expression and Speech under Article 19(1)(a) and Right to Life and Personal Liberty under Article 21 guaranteed by the constitution. The authorities under RTI Act 2005 are called public authorities. The Public Information Authority in the public authorities. The public authorities perform quasi-judicial function of deciding on the application and appeal respectively. This act was enacted in order to consolidate the fundamental right in the Indian Constitution 'freedom of speech'. Since RTI is implicit in the Right to Freedom of Speech and Expression under Article 19 of the Indian Constitution, it is an implied fundamental right.

Information disclosure in India had traditionally been restricted by the Official Secrets Act, 1923 and various other special laws, which the new RTI overrides. Right to Information codifies a fundamental right of the citizens of India. RTI has proven to be extremely useful, but is counteracted by the Whistle Blower's Protection Act, 2011.

The Right to Information (Amendment) Bill, 2019, seeks to amend sections 13, 16, and 27 of the RTI Act. Section 13 of the original Act: It sets the term of the Chief Information Commissioner and Information Commissioners at five years (or until the age of 65, whichever is earlier). Finally, in *Ashwanee K. Singh's* case on 20th September 2020, it is stabilised that right to information is a fundamental right.

The act extends to the whole of India. It covers all the constitutional authorities, including executive, legislature and judiciary; any institution or body established or constituted by an act of Parliament or a state legislature. It is also defined in the Act that bodies or authorities established or constituted by order or notification of appropriate government including bodies "owned, controlled or substantially financed" by government, or non-Government organizations "substantially financed, directly or indirectly by funds".

Right to Information Act (2005) empowers every citizen to: -

1) Ask any questions from the Government or seek any information.
2) Take Copies of any government documents.
3) Inspect any government documents.
4) Take samples of materials of any Government work.

Objectives of the Act: -

a) To empower the citizens
b) To promote transparency and accountability
c) To contain corruption and
d) To enhance people's participation in democratic process.

Reasons for Adoption of Information Act: -

a) Corruption and scandals
b) International pressure and activism
c) Modernization and the information society

Features of the Act

Section 1(2): It extends to the whole of India except the State of Jammu and Kashmir.

Section- 2 (f): "Information" means any material in any form, including Records, Documents, Memos, e-mails, Opinions, Advices, Press releases, Circulars, Orders, Logbooks, Contracts, Reports, Papers, Samples, Models, Data material held in any electronic form and information relating to any private body which can be accessed by a Public Authority under any other law for the time being in force.

Section- 2(j): "Right to Information" means the right to information accessible under this Act which is held by or under the control of **any public authority** and includes the right to:

   (a) Inspection of work, documents, records;

(b) Taking notes, extracts or certified copies of documents or records;

(c) Taking certified samples of material;

(d) Obtaining information in the form of diskettes, floppies, tapes, video cassettes or in any other electronic mode or through printouts where such information is stored in a computer or in any other device.

Section 4 of the RTI Act requires *suo motu* disclosure of information by each public authority. However, such disclosures have remained less than satisfactory.

Section 8 (1) mentions exemptions against furnishing information under RTI Act.

Section 8 (2) provides for disclosure of information exempted under Official Secrets Act, 1923 if larger public interest is served.

The Act also provides for appointment of **Information Commissioners** at Central and State level. Public authorities have designated some of its officers as Public Information Officer. They are responsible to give information to a person who seeks information under the RTI Act.

Time period: In normal course, information to an applicant is to be **supplied within 30 days** from the receipt of application by the public authority.

If information sought **concerns the life or liberty of a person,** it shall be supplied **within 48 hours.**

In case the application is sent through the Assistant Public Information Officer or it is sent to a wrong public authority, five days shall be added to the period of thirty days or 48 hours.

Some Important questions regarding the RTI Act: -

Que) *Are private bodies covered under RTI?*

Ans) Private bodies are not within the Act's in a decision of Sarbjit Roy vs Delhi Electricity Regulatory Commission; the Central Information Commission also reaffirmed that privatised public utility companies fall within the purview of RTI. As of 2014, private institutions and NGO's receiving over 98% of their infrastructure funds from the government come under the Act.

Que) *What is the RTIs stand on political parties?*

Ans) The Central Information Commission held that the political parties are public authorities and are answerable to citizens under the RTI Act. The CIC said that seven national parties- Congress, BJP, NCP, CPI(M), CPI and BSP and BJP- has been substantially funded indirectly by the Central Government and have the character of public authorities under the RTI Act as they perform public functions. But in August 2013 the government introduced a Right to Information (Amendment) Bill which would remove political parties from the scope of the law. Currently no parties are under the RTI Act and a case has been filed for bringing all political parties under it.

Que) *What are the recent amendments in the RTI Act?*

Ans) The Right to Information Act was amended on 25 July, 2019. It was modified in terms and conditions of service of the CIC and other Information Commissioners at the centre and in states. It had been criticised as watering down the independence of the information commissions.

Supreme Court of India on 13th November 2019, upheld the decision of Delhi High Court bringing the office of Chief Justice of India under the purview of Right to Information (RTI) Act.

In recent Years there has been an almost unstoppable global trend towards recognition of the right to information by countries, intergovernmental organisations, civil society, and the people. The right to information has been recognised as a fundamental human right, which upholds the inherent dignity of all human beings. The right to information forms the crucial underpinning of participatory democracy- it is essential to ensure accountability and good governance. Without information, people cannot adequately exercise their rights as citizens or make informed choices.

Factors affecting the free-flow of information in India: -

a) The legislative framework includes several pieces of restrictive legislation, such as the Official Secrets Act, 1923;
b) The pervasive culture of secrecy and arrogance within the bureaucracy; and
c) The low levels of literacy and rights awareness amongst India's people.

The primary power RTI is the fact that it empowers individual citizens to requisition information. Hence, without necessarily forming pressure groups or associations, it puts power directly into the hands of the foundation of democracy- *the citizen*.

The Right to Information Act under constitution and its exception: -

The Right to Information movement began in India with the Mazdoor Kisan Shakti Sangathan (MKSS) movement to bring transparency in village accounts through the demand for minimum wages in rural India. False entries in wage rolls were a sign of increasing corruption in the system, which encouraged MKSS to demand official information recorded in the government files.

The constitution of India does not clearly provide Right to Information. However, the Apex court of the country held in several cases that Right to Information is concerned with the Article 19(1)(a) and Article 21 of the Indian constitution which states freedom of expression and speech and right to life and personal liberty, respectively. In other words, we can say that it (Right to Information) protects the very purpose of the such articles. Article 19 and 21 comes under part 3 of the constitution which is the fundamental Rights of the Indian constitution. In this way we can say that the right to information might be considered as fundamental right of the constitution.

Article 19 of the Constitution of India talks about rights and in Article 19(1) (a) we have the freedom of speech. This freedom not only extends to the right to know. This right to know also has some limitations to it, for say, information of national security or any other matter which would affect the nation's integrity. But if contains information for example related to sanitation then it is not a matter of national security and the public has the right to know why such information is withheld.

Citizens have a right to know about government affairs. However, the right is not absolute; secrecy can be legitimately claimed in respect of transactions with repercussion on public security.

Popular RTI's filed yet: -

Rafael Scandal (alleged) RTI- While reviewing its 2018 judgement in regarding the Rafael Jets, the Supreme Court in response to the arguments being made by the then Attorney General K.K.Venugopal, said; "The RTI Act brought a revolution. In 2009, your own government said file noting can be made available under the RTI. Let us not go back now." The court also said that the RTI filed in this particular case even overrides the Official Secrets Act.

Although, this RTI filed by Former Union Ministers Arun Shourie, Yashvant Sinha and the famed advocate Prashant Bhushan proved futile when the court held its 2018 judgement and gave a clean chit to the Government, but it proved quite successful in reinvigorating people's confidence in India's vibrant democratic structures.

Tukde-Tukde Gang RTI- In January 2020, an activist named Saket Gokhale filed an RTI in the Ministry of Home Affairs questioning about the alleged anti-national squad called *'tukde-tukde gang'*.

The Home Ministry's reply to this query shocked many; it said "The Ministry of Home Affairs has no information concerning Tukde-Tukde gang." Gokhale mentioned in his RTI plea that the Home Minister said while addressing a political rally in Delhi, "tukde-tukde gang needs to be taught a lesson." The continuous efforts by these brave activists to hold the government to account inspires many Indians. Government data shows that the usage of RTI pleas is on the rise.

Pegasus Snoop gate (alleged) RTI- In October 2021; an activist filed an RTI in the Ministry of Home Affairs questioning the usage of Pegasus Spyware manufactured by on any Indian citizens alleged by Amnesty International. The ministry of Home Affairs replied, "It is informed that no such information is available with the undersigned CPIO." The ministry said that it has no information regarding the alleged snooping of journalists and activists and top politicians including Congress leader Rahul Gandhi and election strategist and Mamta Bannerjee aide, Prashant Kishore.

The allegation comes after Facebook-owned WhatsApp accused Israel-based NSO Group of using the spyware called 'Pegasus' to target over 1,400 WhatsApp users, a few of them in India. As per the instant messaging app, the spyware targeted victims by giving missed calls on their mobile phones.

PM Cares Fund RTI- As the first wave of Coronavirus outbreak wreaked havoc in India, Prime Minister Narendra Modi asked the country to donate generously in the PM-Cares Fund a newly created fund to help for the purchase of medical equipment which was in a short supply in the country. Many asked what the need for a PM Cares Fund is when the Prime Minister's National Relief Fund was already in place. An activist filed a RTI request in April, 2020 enquiring about the allegedly dubious PM Cares Fund in PMO. However, the Prime Minister's Office blocked the request and refused to give any answers to questions, like- What is the total amount collected in the PM Cares Fund? What medical equipment was purchased by the money collected? etc. The government's attitude in this case did nothing but fuelled speculations.

Aarogya Setu Application RTI- At the height of Coronavirus infections in India, the union government launched the Aarogya Setu mobile application for individuals to enable them to track Covid- 19 cases near them. The mobile application was heavily promoted by the government. An RTI Activist Saurav Das filed RTI request in the Ministry of Electronics to enquire about the maker of the app. The Ministry of Electronics replied that it has no information regarding the manufacturer of the app. This triggered a backlash from the civil society and the government's mandate for the government employees to download the app was removed.

Attacks on RTI activists and protection suggestion

Commonwealth Human Rights Initiative (CHRI) data points to over 310 cases across India where people were either attacked, murdered, physically or mentally harassed or had their property damaged because of the information they sought under RTI. The data throws up over 50 alleged murders and two suicides that were directly linked with RTI applications filed. R.T.I. Act 2005 applies to both central as well as state governments. It also covers the acts and functionaries of the public authorities.

There is a consensus felt that there is a need to amend the RTI Act to provide for the protection of those seeking information under the act. The Asian Centre for Human Rights recommends that a separate chapter, "Protection of those seeking information under the (RTI) Act", be inserted into the Act.

Protection measures suggested include:

- Mandatory, immediate registration of complaints of threats or attacks against RTI activists on the First Information Report and placing such FIRs before the magistrate or judge of the area within 24 hours for issuance of directions for protection of those under threats and their family members, and periodic review of such protection measures

- Conducting inquiry into threats or attacks by a police officer not below the rank of Deputy Superintendent of Police /Assistant Commissioner of Police to be concluded within ninety days and we also use RTI and get its benefit.

Issues with the RTI Act, 2005: -

a) Information commissioners do not have adequate authorities to enforce the RTI Act.
b) In case of award of compensation to activist by public authority as ordered by commission, compliance cannot be secured.
c) Poor record-keeping practices
d) Lack of adequate infrastructure and staff for running information commissions.
e) Dilution of supplementary laws like the Whistleblowers Protection Act.

Amendments in the Act, 2019: -

RTI amendment bill was introduced in the Lok Sabha by the Minister of State for Personnel Public Grievances and Pensions on July 19, 2019 and passed on July 22, 2019. It was passed by the Rajya Sabha on July 25, 2019.

Key highlights of the RTI Amendment Act, 2019: -

Term- In 2005 Act, the term for the Central Chief Information Commissioner, State-level Chief Information Commissioner and Information Commissioners was fixed for the term of 5 years (or until the age of 65 years whichever is earlier). But the amendment specifies that the appointment will be for such term as may be prescribed by the central government.

Salary- In the RTI Act, 2005 the salary of the Central Information Commissioner (CIC) was equivalent to the salary of the Chief Election Commissioner, salary of the State Chief Information Commissioner (SCIC) and the Information Commissioners (ICs) was equivalent to the salary of the Election Commissioners and at the state level, State Information Commissioner (SIC) the salary was equivalent Chief Secretary to the state. In this proposal, however, it is suggested that the provisions of the RTI Act, 2005 be amended to provide that the term of office and the salaries, allowances and other terms and conditions of service of, the Chief Information Commissioner and Information Commissioners and the State Chief Information Commissioner and the State Information

Commissioners, shall be such as may be prescribed by the central government.

The main aim of the RTI Act, 2005 which was to promote transparency, accountability in the working of every public authority and the citizens' right to secure the access to information is being crippled by this amendment bill, 2019. This is an attempt to take away the free flow of unbiased information and place before the general public, the filtered information by the public authorities in order to please the government. The government has weakened the sunshine law without providing any credible rationale for bringing an amendment as this will definitely hamper the independent working of the Information Commissioners. They are now no more vested with the independence, transparency, status, and authority but will now be functioning as one of the departments answerable ultimately to the central government.

Head Quarters of the Central Information
Commission.

Bibliography

Acharya, A. (2021) 'Political Theory: An Introduction' (Pearson India Education Services, Noida, U.P.).

Brown, C. (2004) 'Understanding International Relations' (Palgrave Macmillan).

Hague, R. (2004) 'Comparative Government and Politics' (Palgrave Macmillan).

Ghai, K.K (2018) 'ISC Political Science' (Kalyani Publications).

Heywood, A. (2004) 'Political Theory: An Introduction' (Palgrave Macmillan).

Lowe, N. (2013) 'Mastering Modern World History' (Palgrave Macmillan).

Heywood, A. (2017) 'Political Ideologies: An Introduction' (Palgrave Macmillan).

Laxmikanth, M. (2020) 'Indian Polity' (McGraw Hill).

About the Author

Hasan Razi Kazmi is a graduate in Political Science from the University of Delhi, with a keen interest in exploring the complexities of governance and policy making. Born in Lucknow, India, Kazmi's fascination with history and political theory has been shaped by his family's involvement in the Indian Freedom Struggle.

On a personal note, Kazmi has faced significant challenges in his journey as a writer. The loss of his beloved grandfather, his Nana, has been a profound blow. His grandfather was also his closest friend and confidant. Despite this difficult period, he found solace in writing, and pouring his emotions and intellect into this book. He dedicates this work to his grandfather's memory, whose love, guidance, and inspiration continue to shape his thoughts and aspirations.

Through his studies and social interactions, he has developed a passion for understanding the dynamics of power, diplomacy, and social movements. His work seeks to contribute to the ongoing conversations in political theory, international relations, and governance, with a focus on exploring innovative solutions to contemporary challenges.

In this book, Kazmi shares his perspectives on the intricate relationships between political ideologies, international relations, and policy making. With a commitment to critical thinking and nuanced analysis, he aims to engage readers in a thoughtful exploration of the complex issues shaping our world.

Notes

Notes

Notes

Notes

Notes